CONTENTS

Preface

As Director of the Office of Stewardship in Mission Planning, I am very pleased to recommend this work of Maurice Coombs to you, the reader. Maurice has been a friend and colleague of mine in Philadelphia for many years. He is one of the most dedicated and gifted parish clergy I know. His excellent preaching, teaching and writing skills caused me to ask him to be a presenter at two of our regional stewardship meetings and at three of our planned giving gatherings. In these stewardship educational contexts, Maurice articulately developed his theological and biblical approach to stewardship. I am pleased with this written version of what I had heard previously.

My wish is that you will find in Maurice's words a channel of God's grace to encourage you to be a faithful, responsible and generous Christian steward.

The Rev. Ronald L. Reed
Director of Stewardship
Mission Planning Unit
Episcopal Church Center

Introduction

Much of this monograph was prepared for presentation as a Bible study/theological reflection for Regional Training Conferences sponsored by the Office of Stewardship of the Presiding Bishop.

The substance has been read by many people who have made suggestions and criticisms. Those suggestions have been incorporated into this revision of the original studies.

I would like to take as my own some words of Dietrich Ritschl, former Professor of Systematic Theology at the University of Heidelberg when he wrote that *I am one of those who takes no delight in opening up divides and establishing fronts, and I know of no even ostensible obligation towards the truth which calls me to do that. And I am all the more curious to find ways into the depths of the logical and theological bases for what believers say and for responsible guidelines for our action.*[1]

I welcome dialogue on the substance of this exploration.

Maurice A. Coombs
Philadelphia Pa.
Lent 1988

WHICH THEOLOGY?

For centuries the Episcopal Church, as part of the church catholic, has held tenaciously to a simple formula whereby truth may be divined. Not Truth (with a capital T), the whole truth and nothing but the truth. That Truth is incarnated in the person of Jesus of Nazareth who said of himself, *I am the Way, the Truth and the Life.*[2] The truth we are looking for here is the validity of lifestyle that approaches, as far as humanly possible, the will and intention of God for the human family. To discover that truth three realities of our experience must be held in constant tension. The three realities are Scripture, Tradition and Reason.

• Scripture: Because it is the primary witness to the Word of God, which Word is defined in the Collect for the Second Sunday in Lent as a prayer to God that humanity *embrace and hold fast the unchange-able truth of thy Word, Jesus Christ.*[3] William Countryman, however, reminds us that: *God speaks to us through the Word of Scripture. Yet...it is not always easy to hear what God is saying. The difficulties arise from the limitations of human speech, of writing, of our created nature (which prohibits any kind of static perfection), and also from our own unreadiness to hear. Reading and listening to the Bible, then, calls for knowledge, skill, and devotion. Our reward is to be freed from the present so that we can go out on pilgrimage toward what God wills us to become.*[4]

• Tradition: Because, for centuries, communities within the human family have been shaped by Scripture. There are those who would argue that the communities also helped to shape the Scripture, but that leads us into another issue. Episcopalians recognize and respect Tradition. Some go as far as to place it on the same level as the sacred text itself. It is sad that some 20th century Christians work on the assumption that they are the first people ever to read the Bible, and any suggestion that Tradition may throw some light on what it means to be a Christian is met with utter disdain.

1

• Reason: Because Episcopalians believe that God endowed us with the ability to think, analyze, criticize, define and interpret data whether the data be experience or Scripture. By using our powers of reason we are able to tell the true from the false, the light from the dark, the good from the evil.

All three, Scripture, Tradition and Reason, are essential in the search for truth and all three must be held in constant tension. They are the three legs of the stool of truth and without all three the stool will not be kept in balance.

All Christians are theologians. In fact, given the strict definition of theology as the "science of divine things," all human beings are theologians. Even Marxists are theologians. For them "divine" has no capital "D" but principles like economic determinism and dialectical materialism are seen to be forces "outside the individual" which control life and its living. Others believe in the stars. The writers of the Declaration of Independence believed in "nature," "providence," and "nature's God." The hundreds of thousands who play the slot machines or the tables in casinos believe in chance or luck. Everyone is a theologian, everyone has a belief system where the dominating feature is something or someone outside, beyond.

Christians are theologians who believe that the will of God has been revealed and focused in the life, teaching, death and resurrection of Jesus of Nazareth. Revelation is one part of discernment of the will of God. The other is our capacity to make deductions based on experience as to the most effective way to behave as human beings. There are examples of theophany, a direct revelation, but these are the exception, not the rule.

I sometimes think of myself as a conductor reaching toward a current of electricity coming toward me. At an infinitesimal gap the current leaps in a blazing spark. That is the moment of truth, the "aha!" moment, when theology ceases to be something I read about in musty tomes and becomes the very fabric of my life.

In the introduction to his book, *Stages of Faith*, James Fowler wrote these harrowing words which illustrate what I mean:

2

Four a.m. in the darkness of a cold winter morning, suddenly I am fully and frighteningly awake. I see it clearly. I am going to die. This body, this mind, this lived and living myth, this husband, father, teacher, son, friend, will cease to be. The tide of life which propels me with such force will cease and I — this "I" taken so much for granted by me—will no longer walk this earth... "Real life" suddenly feels like a transient dream. In the strange aloneness of this moment, defined by the certainty of death, I awake to the true facts of life.

In that moment of unprecedented aloneness experienced in my thirty-third year, I found myself staring into the abyss of mystery that surrounds our lives. As never before I found myself asking, "When all these persons, and relations and projects that shape and fill my life are removed, who or what is left? When this biological embodiment of me ceases to function, is there —will there be — any "I"? When the "I" that is me steps into the velvet darkness, will there be this center of consciousness, this "I am" or not? And if so by whom will I be met?"

Had you met me on the day before this happened you would have come to know one who understood himself—and was understood by others — as a man of faith. A Christian, a minister, a teacher of theology, a counselor, yes, even a witness for his faith. But in the distancing of that strange awakening my faith...seemed remote and detached from me... During those moments I was not in my faith. I seemed to stand completely naked—a soul without a body, raiment, relationships or roles. A soul alone with—with what? With whom?[5]

Theology, for the Christian, is the science of the ultimate. We accept that there is empirical evidence for the existence of God and evidence that God has revealed his intention. Christian theology is a system of codifying that intention into a pattern of belief and action which will ensure that God's will is *done on earth as it is in heaven.*[6]

It is obvious that Christian theology is not uniform. Even in rigidly totalitarian systems questioning and debate have not been suppressed. A Magisterium may well deny a forum in which to ask questions and debate theology but it has not, and cannot, silence the questions or stop the debate.

Reflecting on the theology of stewardship must begin with the question, "which theology?" Probably we would all like to answer that with the assertion that what we want is "biblical theology." Some would temper that with a willingness to look at the "process" by which the science of God in the pages of Scripture has shaped, and been shaped by, the experience of the church as a living community throughout the last 2,000 years. For these people this body of Tradition has the same value as the words of the text. Some others feel a profound confidence in the reasoning processes with which the Creator has endowed human beings. Reason demands a critical approach to both Scripture and Tradition. Some would test a belief system by looking at what it produces. Results prove validity.

Beware of false prophets who come to you disguised as sheep but underneath are ravenous wolves. You will be able to tell them by their fruits. Can people pick grapes from thorns, or figs from thistles?[7]

Jesus of Nazareth sees results as at least one test of the validity of theology.

We are being told constantly by the media pundits that "fundamentalism" is rapidly becoming the preferred theology of American Christians. They point to the increases in fundamentalist churches and contrast them to the decline in the so-called mainline churches. Fundamentalism believes that theology is a "given." Divine intention is clearly spelled out in Scripture and Scripture is infallible and inerrant. Fundamentalists have created "Bible-believing churches" where the belief system for congregants is set and unalterable. Throughout its history Anglicanism has faced this attempt to define theology and has always maintained that Scripture, Tradition and Reason are the only reliable bases for a sound theology and all three must be held in tension. Scripture, Tradition, or Reason alone will produce a warped theology, a belief system that will be sinful because it misses the mark of Divine intention.

Biblical fundamentalism will lose its allure, as it always has, because a great many of its adherents will see that it brings a "worldview" to the Scripture, rather than receiving a worldview *from* Scripture. Anglicanism will be called on to pick up the pieces of

4

fractured lives and provide a coherent theology to give hope for the future.

We will look at stewardship through the lenses of Scripture, Tradition and Reason, which, like the blue, red and green lenses of a TV projector will give us an integrated image in "living color!" That metaphor reminds me of seeing some of those enormous projection TVs in stores where the balance of red, blue and green was not right and the picture was dreadful. To compensate for the imbalance, and the apparent unwillingness of some viewers to adjust the set manually, most "state of the art" television sets have a built-in color balance control. Because Christian reflection takes place in the context of worship and fellowship we will need to rely heavily on the control of the Holy Spirit to keep the image in balance. I doubt there is anyone who wants an image of stewardship to be totally red or even blue.

The Rev'd John MacNaughton in his book *More Blessed to Give* describes a Peanuts cartoon where Lucy and Linus are in the house looking out the window in a heavy rain storm. Lucy says, *Boy, look at it rain. What if it floods the whole world?" To which Linus replies, "It will never do that. In the ninth chapter of Genesis God promised Noah that would never happen again, and the sign of the promise is the rainbow." Lucy is reassured and smiles, saying, "You've taken a great load off my mind." To which Linus replies, "Sound theology has a way of doing that."* MacNaughton goes on to make the comment that: *The basic questions of life will ultimately be satisfied only by theological answers. This includes questions about money and our use of it.*[8]

Which theological answers? Professor Alan Richardson pointed out that:

In essence and in origin...Christian faith is not ideological, but to assert that is not to deny that in any given age it expresses itself in the ideological forms of the times...Too often the different aspects of historical development, such as the economic or the religious, are studied in separate compartments; in particular the history of Christian thought has all too frequently been written in abstraction from the broad current of social, political and economic history with which it is so closely interrelated...there is an important connection between religious and ideological factors in the mind of the sixteenth and seventeenth centuries... an Arminian theology is better suited to the social needs of the older landed aristocracy, while the vigorous and expanding bourgeois classes found more adequate expression for their ideological standpoint in the theology of Calvanistic Puritanism.[9]

Some years ago when I was serving as Domestic Chaplain to the Most Rev'd George Appleton, the then Anglican Archbishop in Jerusalem, we met with His Beatitude Pimen, the Patriarch of Moscow. The Archbishop quizzed the Patriarch on his apparent ability to exercise Christian ministry in a context of state ownership of the means of production, distribution and exchange — socialism. The Patriarch of Moscow could not see any conflict at all. For him the ideology of the state was not an inhibiting factor in the stewardship of Christians belonging to the Russian Orthodox Church. When the Rev'd Billy Graham made a similar statement following a visit to Russia and some of its satellites he was pilloried by the Western press.

Bishop Desmond Tutu was in Canada a few years ago, attending the meeting of the Central Committee of the World Council of Churches. He is reported to have called the capitalism of South Africa "horrendous" and declared himself to be a socialist. The New York Times for Saturday, August 23, 1986, reported that the Bishop reiterated that opinion on his return from a visit to China.

President Reagan occasionally made statements which seemed to equate capitalism and free enterprise with God's will and intention for human society. In this ideological struggle protagonists on both sides called the other system names, like "evil empire." The thawing of the cold war has seen the name-calling virtually cease.

For the past eight or nine years I have worked with parish vestries to help them compose a "theological statement of stewardship" for their parish. Inevitably, a stewardship statement will contain the assertion that everything we own is a *gift from God*. God OWNS everything. Theocratic socialism par excellence! The statement will then go on to say that we "give back to God" what is already his. The

6

words have a nice ring to them and they make us feel very comfortable when we express them. I wonder if they are sound theology.

I am convinced that when God gave humanity the gift of the earth he gave up ownership of it. God is not an "Indian giver." When the Psalmist cries *To Yahweh belong earth and all it holds, the world and all who live in it,*[10] he overlooks the Scripture which states that the title to much of creation has been transferred to human beings. That transfer of title is on record in Genesis where, after creating male and female God blessed them, saying to them,

Be fruitful, multiply, fill the earth and conquer it. Be masters of the fish of the sea, the birds of heaven and all living animals on the earth. God said, See, I give you all the seed bearing plants that are upon the whole earth, and all the trees with seed bearing fruit; this shall be your food. To all wild beasts, all birds of heaven and all living reptiles on the earth I give all the foliage of plants for food. And so it was. God saw all he had made, and indeed it was very good.[11]

God has given the earth away. It is ours to conquer, to use or to abuse.

Professor Bernard W. Anderson claims that *the announcement that in Christ God has turned the world over to men is consistent with the biblical creation-faith as expressed in the Old Testament, especially in Genesis 1 and Psalm 8. Man is crowned with the supreme honor of being the agent who "subdues" the earth (Gen. 1:28), who exerts "dominion" over "all things" (Ps 8:6). God has given man responsibility for the world. In a limited sense, he is intended to be a king who, in the ceaseless conflict of history, helps to sustain the creation in the face of the menacing powers of chaos.*[12]

Professor Frank Stagg points out that *God made man in his own likeness able to love or to hate, trust or distrust, live under the sovereignty of God or rebel. Man can say "yes" or "no" to God, and in so doing he is not merely repeating words God puts in his mouth. God was free enough to give man freedom; and the freedom, once given is real.*[13] He goes on to point out that the *ultimate dominion for God and for man is that of love — persuasive power but not coercive*

7

power. God's dominion is not tyranny of man nor nature. Man's proper dominion is never tyranny but that of the power of responsible love.[14] Stagg has another observation which is worth more than a passing glance: *the wrath of God means that God takes man's freedom so seriously that he permits man to self destruct if man so chooses.*"[15] Another great Christian scholar reinforces my theme here when he writes that: *Perhaps the most satisfying of the many interpretations, both ancient and modern, of the meaning of the image of God in man is that which sees it basically as responsibility.*[16]

I am proposing that the theology of stewardship begins with the assertion that we own the earth, we human beings individually and collectively. The title has been transferred to us; it is not held by a bank called "God" who will repossess it if we don't keep up the payments. What we do with that gift is our individual and collective responsibility. That is what God intended and we can't shirk our responsibility for the maintenance of the earth by saying that it belongs to God and he should look after it!

We all have heard the cry, when great tragedy strikes, "Why did God allow this to happen?" It's as nonsensical as saying to someone who gave you a priceless vase as a gift "why did you let that happen?" when through carelessness you drop the vase on the kitchen floor. The giver gave the thing to you and it is your responsibility, not the giver's, to care for it!

That's where I begin in trying to discover a theology of stewardship. We will go on to see how that fundamental premise of personal and collective right and responsibility is exercised as human beings attempted to define their response to God's audacious gift.

Paul wrote, *There is nothing to boast about in anything human: Paul, Apollos, Cephas (Peter), the world, life and death, the present and the future, are all your servants; but you belong to Christ and Christ belongs to God.*[17]

Canon J. B. Phillips in his transliteration of Paul's letters[18] puts "everything is yours!" for the Jerusalem Bible's "are all your servants." The New English Bible says "all of them belong to you;" the Revised Standard Version, "all are yours," which is the translation in the Living Bible and the King James Version.

The K.J.V. and the other translations are explicit in making all things our property. Even the modified Jerusalem Bible's translation of "all your servants" denotes ownership because servants were property!

The Genesis passage I referred to earlier gave the ownership of plant and animal life into the hands of human beings. Paul goes even further and gives us the world, life, death, present and future. We own it all. But the incarnation, God becoming human in Jesus of Nazareth, creates a "limited partnership" in which we also recognize that we belong to Jesus and Jesus belongs to God.

The apostles recognized that within that limited partnership human beings "owned" property and resources. Luke's account of the attempted fraud of Ananias and Sapphira contains the bold assertion, *while you still owned the land, wasn't it yours to keep, and after you had sold it, wasn't the money yours to do with as you liked?*[19]

A Christian theology of stewardship accepts that the world, its means of production, distribution and exchange, belong to the human race. But the human race has been purchased by Jesus of Nazareth and Jesus of Nazareth has given it back to God. A valid theology of stewardship will build from that premise and seek to work out how that trinity of ownership is exercised.

The Hebrews had a system which recognized their property rights and responsibilities. They called it the tithe.[20]

The tithe was paid by the owners in order that their primary function as human beings, the worship of God, might be carried out in a fitting manner. The tithe supported an organization of people, program and property in order that the worship of God be available to the people.

But the tithe was only one of the responsibilities. The Jews also had to give alms to the poor. They also had to pay taxes to the state and to the Temple.

We have added another vehicle through which we attempt to discharge our responsibilities for the "all things" we own. We call it the "pledge." As we go on we will reflect on what these things mean in our free enterprise society.

A theology of stewardship, if it is truly biblical, will be true to the intention of God for his family. But it will also be true to the unique

9

place in the created order God has given to human beings. God has made humanity *little less than a god and crowned him with glory and splendor, made him lord over the work of your hands, set all things under his feet.*[21] Such an exalted position demands more than lip service to the rights and responsibilities involved!

RESPONSIBLE STEWARDSHIP
1

I first heard the phrase "holy worldliness" in the early 1960s. It was used by Hans-Ruedi Weber,[22] an extraordinary layman who, at that time, was Associate Director of the Ecumenical Institute, Bossey, Switzerland.

The idea of holy worldliness shocked me to the core. I began my Christian pilgrimage in a church where we were told constantly that the "world" was evil and we were exhorted to shun the world. Worldly people smoked, drank (alcohol), danced, went to the movies, gambled, played cards and, horror of horrors, had sex outside marriage! The image was of two globes. On the left was the world, on which was superimposed a serpent, the Hebraic symbol of evil. On the right was the church (ours of course!), on which was superimposed a cross, the Christian symbol of good. Between the globes a "great gulf was fixed." You either lived in one world or the other.

In my teens I began to wonder about all that. But this formative teaching about the evil world had so conditioned me that I was repelled by the idea of holy worldliness.

Much of that teaching can be traced back to St. Augustine[23] and his "twin cities" view of creation. The tenacity of this approach is obvious with the current emphasis on so-called "secular humanism," roundly condemned by fundamentalists.

Despite the condemnation of the Manichean heresy,[24] vestiges of this dualism remain. If I am honest with myself I admit that some of that early teaching sticks with me. Isn't the idea of an "evil world" at the root of my suspicion of genetic engineering? Somehow I haven't come to grips emotionally with my intellectual confidence that the title deed for the world has been given by the Creator to the creation. That is an issue of my pilgrimage toward what God wills me to become which has yet to move from my head to my heart!

I have suggested that a theology of stewardship which is faithful to the Anglican expression of the faith catholic will involve holding the tension between Scripture, Tradition and Reason. We use the term

11

"stewardship" when we talk about the relationship of things to self and God. I would prefer "theology of ownership," but I suspect that to use it would be as repulsive to many now as "holy worldliness" was to me when I first heard it! I doubt that the same feeling would arise, though, from using the term "responsible ownership!"

 The word "stewardship" occurs in the Bible only four times. Three of the occurrences are in the fascinating story Jesus told of the "unjust steward."[25] The New English Bible uses "manager" rather than steward. The Living Bible calls the fellow an "accountant." In my library I have several dictionaries of the New Testament. The word "stewardship" is not found in any of them! The story Jesus told of the shrewd fellow who was discovered mismanaging his boss' property and the verses following (Luke 16:9-12) are fraught with difficulties of interpretation. Whatever it all means it seems to be a very meager text from which to elevate the word "stewardship" to such a lofty height in our church vocabulary!

The only other occurrence of "stewardship,"[26] at least in the Revised Standard Version, gives us a little more to go on. St. Paul assumes that the Ephesian Christians have "heard of the stewardship of God's grace that was given to me for you." The K.J.V. writes of the "dispensation of the grace of God," The Living Bible "that God has given me this special work of showing God's favor to you Gentiles," The New English Bible "God has assigned me the gift of his grace." J. B. Phillips writes, "God gave me grace to become your minister," and the Jerusalem Bible translates stewardship as "I have been entrusted by God with the grace he meant for you." Here there is no confusion between ownership and stewardship. Only God can own his grace! "Holy worldliness" will mean that I accept his grace and use it rightly to enjoy the world and all that is in it, which he has given to me to own.

The commandment "You shall not steal"[27] is absurd if the people to whom it was addressed did not have the right to own anything. The Hebrews are the first group in biblical history to lay down laws about the rights and responsibilities of ownership. But ownership preceded the laws of Leviticus and Deuteronomy. The Genesis writer records that Abram was a very rich man, with livestock, silver and gold.[28]

12

It is in the saga of father Abraham that we have the first mention of the tithe when he gave to Melchizedek, the king of Salem who was a "priest of God Most High," a tithe of everything he had captured from the four great kings.[29]

It would be both boring and redundant to go over all the texts which relate to the tithe as a responsibility coupled with the right of ownership of the means of production, distribution and exchange God had given to the human family, typified in the Hebrew nation. I want to move on to the place of the tithe in Christian understanding of rights and responsibilities. But before we do that I want to take up another, to me, misleading emphasis which has become normative in our stewardship education. It is the often stated idea that what we give (tithe or not) is given to God.

I wonder if the reason much of our stewardship exhortation is rejected is simply because it has the appearance of sophistry! I am well aware of passages like the sermon prayer of David on the building of the Temple.[30] It is disturbing that the simplistic, anthropomorphic language of that sermon is used uncritically to give biblical basis to the idea that we give to God. The people and David and Solomon gave to a structure and an institution — the Temple — and all its departments and programs; they did not give anything to God. God doesn't *need* anything; God only *wants*, and the only thing God wants is my love, the responsible use of my life and the world he has deeded to me.

But my parish *needs*, so does the diocese, the national church and the agencies and institutions we have set up to perform ministry and enable others to discharge, in a fully human way, their rights and responsibilities for what they have. I need to learn to be a "responsible prodigal," not be told that what I have isn't mine or that somehow I'm able to give my Father anything except my love.[31]

I ponder, and I ask you to ponder, whether we might use terms like "giving to God" with not a little hope that the latent "fear of God" we assume is still operating may not help to loosen the purse strings!

Bonhoeffer touched a profound truth when he wrote in *Letters and Papers from Prison* that *I have come to appreciate the 'worldliness' of Christianity as never before.* [That] *the Christian is not a 'homo religiousus' but a man, pure and simple*... It seems to me we need to address that humanity in our theology of stewardship with more clarity than simply telling people they are giving their money, or time, or talent to God.

I have attempted to show that we human beings have been given the right of ownership of the world. I have stressed that a Christian sees that right as mystically involved with our belonging to Jesus of Nazareth and of Jesus belonging to God. That trinity of corporate ownership carries with it rights and responsibilities. One of the responsibilities is to see that provision is made both for the worship of God, the only thing we can give him, and the ministry to all humanity, which involves helping them to be reconciled to this partnership and work effectively within it to ensure that God's will is done "on earth as it is in heaven."

I have briefly mentioned the "tithe." The word appears in only three places in the New Testament and in all three the context is in relation to the Hebraic system.[32] I take issue with John MacNaughton when he writes that *tithing is seldom mentioned in the New Testament because, in Jesus' mind, it was simply assumed as normal and expected. It was so obvious a standard that it was beyond the need of discussion.*[33]

Jesus' "mind," in direct expression, is recorded only in the gospels and once in Acts where Jesus is reported to have said *it is more blessed to give than to receive.*[34]

I am not so sure that this argument from silence can be applied to the rest of the New Testament, to the responsibilities of the post resurrection — particularly gentile — Christians.

We know that Jesus paid the tithe and he paid the Temple tax, once miraculously.[35]

It is almost certain he would also have paid his taxes to the Romans. How did he do all that? Did he have an inheritance from Joseph? Judas apparently was the treasurer of Jesus' traveling minyan. Were contributions collected from friends and relatives to cover expenses? To whom did Jesus pay his tithe?" Joachim Jeremias[36] gives a picture of Jerusalem in Jesus' day and, from writings of the period, explains that the tithes were paid to the Levites and the priests. But he makes the observation that *even Philo, who paints a glowing picture of the*

14

rich revenues of the priests in order to prove the splendor of the Mosaic Law, had to admit that the priests would have had plenty if everyone had paid his full dues, but in fact they had been reduced to poverty, because 'some of the people' (an obvious understatement) were indifferent.[37] The argument that the tithe is not mentioned elsewhere in the New Testament because everybody did it is fragile.

In the immediate post resurrection period the "followers of the way" of Jesus of Nazareth were expected to give up everything they owned: *The faithful all lived together and owned everything in common; they sold their goods and possessions and shared out the proceeds among themselves according to what each one needed.*[38]

Jeremias has a helpful note on this practice:

Common ownership in the primitive Church has been a matter of considerable controversy. The reasons that are cited against it do not seem to me to be convincing, providing it is remembered that the participation was voluntary. The fact that only one example, that of Joseph Barnabas (Acts 4:36f.) is given is explained by his importance. The privately owned house in Acts 12:12f. was obviously the place of assembly for the community. The existence of poverty in the community is explicable (Acts 6:1ff.) if the common ownership extended to landed property. Whoever doubts the accounts of the primitive 'communism' must offer an explanation of how they arose.[39]

This practice, which is better labeled "commonism" rather than communism, for obvious reasons, apparently applied only to the Jerusalem community. With the expansion of the church into the gentile world this Jerusalem practice seems not to have been a prerequisite of becoming a Christian. It is also obvious that the Jerusalem Christians had little or no resources to tithe. I doubt that tithing was prescribed for gentile Christians. It is stretching the argument from silence to the breaking point to suggest that we have no record of tithing because it was common practice.

Although tithing was not unique to the Hebrews, having been used by Persians, Romans and Greeks, among others, even given that background I doubt that all the gentile converts would automatically tithe. Certainly the Jewish practice of tithing was not demanded, as can be seen from the letter sent from the Jerusalem Church to the gentile converts:

It has been decided by the Holy Spirit and by ourselves not to saddle you with any burden beyond these essentials: you are to abstain from food sacrificed to idols, from blood, from the meat of strangled animals and from fornication. Avoid these, and you will do what is right.[40]

The Episcopal Church, through its General Convention, has affirmed the tithe as the minimum standard of giving. Our right to do that is not in question. What I have attempted to show is that the biblical tithe cannot be used to support that standard. The biblical tithe was a tax pure and simple. To mix "tithing" with "giving" is to mix apples and oranges.

If that is true, what are we left with in trying to discover a responsible stewardship? Or, if the tithe is to be expected, with all its biblical associations, where does that leave voluntary giving? Sometimes to embark on a reflection of the theology of stewardship raises more questions than it answers.[41]

RESPONSIBLE STEWARDSHIP
2

I have attempted to show that a biblical theology of responsible stewardship (or as I would prefer, responsible ownership) must not confuse tithing with voluntary giving. I have some ideas about the practical implications of this theological approach, but before we can come to that we need to spend some time on the matter of almsgiving.

In the economic environment in which Jesus lived, acts of charity played an important part in Jewish piety. There was a Jerusalem proverb which went, "Acts of kindness are the salt of wealth." The Jewish historian, Josephus, writes of the charity of Herod at the time of the great famine in 25-24 B.C.

In the first place, to those who were able to provide food for themselves by their own labor he distributed grain in very exact proportions. Then, since there were many who, because of old age or some other attendant infirmity, were unable to prepare the grain for themselves, he provided for them by putting bakers to work, and furnishing them with food already prepared. He also took care that they should go through the winter without danger [to health], including that of being in need of clothing, for their flocks had been destroyed and completely consumed, so that they had no wool to use or any other material for covering themselves.[42]

The "food cupboard," "soup kitchen" and Goodwill Store have a long history! The noble families of Jerusalem recognized their responsibility to the poor went beyond the tithe they paid to the religious establishment or the taxes they paid to the government.

Two, the religious institutions had welfare systems. Their social services were somewhere between the private and public services. Jeremias points out that the Essenes, a religious sect which had repudiated the orthodoxy of the Temple establishment, had in each city their own agents who provided their travelers with clothing and other necessities.[43]

Besides those who were poor because of circumstances, there were those who chose poverty.

The first beatitude has to do with the poor, but Matthew and Luke record it differently. Luke writes that Jesus said *how happy are you who are poor: yours is the kingdom of God.*[44] Matthew has Jesus say *how happy are the poor in spirit: theirs is the kingdom of heaven.*[45]

What does Jesus mean? Is he saying that poverty is the ideal state of life?

Luke's "you who are poor" forces us to ask who the "you" are to whom Jesus is speaking. If you back up a bit in the text, to Luke's introduction of the sermon, he writes of Jesus: *Then fixing his eyes on his disciples he said...*[46]

Both Matthew and Luke set the sermon in the context of a vast crowd. Matthew doesn't discriminate between the crowd and the disciples in the way Luke does. This is important. Luke sees Jesus speaking only to the disciples as the "you who are poor" while Matthew with his "poor in spirit" assumes Jesus is talking to the whole crowd.

In the world of the Greeks, the Romans and the Jews, Jesus' world, at the low end of the scale were those who begged for a living. There were others who were also classified as poor but who worked for a living. Long before Jesus' time it was thought that being wealthy was the best way to become virtuous, but by the time Jesus began to teach in Palestine it was being argued that poverty seemed to lead people to acquire culture and this would lead to virtue, so poverty may well be a good thing. It is interesting that Luke has Jesus follow the four beatitudes with four castigations the first of which is *But alas for you who are rich: you are having your consolation now.*[47]

When Jesus is speaking about poverty to the disciples he is speaking about those who have no property. Certainly if you were to be a full time disciple you had to give up your wealth! The Bhagwan in Oregon convinced many young Americans of that only a few years ago. The difference is that Jesus' disciples were called to surrender their wealth and give it to the poor. The Bhagwan apparently wanted the wealth for himself.

18

Matthew broadens the issue considerably by introducing the "poor in spirit." One translation has Jesus say *Fortunate are the humble in spirit, for theirs is the kingdom of heaven.*[48]

That rendering is similar to a saying in the Dead Sea Scroll, the Qumran War Scroll: *Blessed be the Lord God of Israel...giving... vigor to the shoulders of the bowed, and...to the lowly spirits; firmness to the melting heart.*[49]

So the disciple must let go all wealth[50] but ordinary folk need the poverty of spirit. The poverty Matthew speaks of is that of a person who is fully conscious of the poverty of all human resource, who knows his need and desire for God.

Canon J. B. Phillips, in his transliteration of the gospels makes the distinction very clear. He puts the Matthew beatitude as *How happy are those who know their need for God, for the kingdom of Heaven is theirs,* but renders Luke as, *How happy are you who own nothing, for the kingdom of God is yours.*

This is no mere distinction without a difference. It has important implications for the church's teaching on stewardship. The demand for discipleship was total poverty. In the first generation of the church that demand was exerted on all who wanted to become "followers of the way." Luke asserts this "commonism," as we have already seen. *The faithful all lived together and owned everything in common; they sold their goods and possessions and shared out the proceeds among themselves according to what each one needed.*[51]

When Barnabas, a Cypriot Jew, joined the apostolic band he owned land, presumably on Cyprus, but he sold it and brought the money and presented it to the Apostles.[52]

The story of Annanias and Sapphira,[53] who tried to "hedge their bets," shows that in the beginning becoming a disciple involved total poverty. Apparently the principle did not last. But the notion that poverty was the Christian way par excellence gave rise to monasticism. For centuries there were two classes of Christians. First class were the monastics who took the vow of poverty, and second class were all the rest.

The Reformation repudiated this two class system. Deitrich Bonhoeffer wrote that *Luther's return from the cloister to the world was the worst blow the world has suffered since the days of early*

Christianity...Hitherto the Christian life had been the achievement of a few choice spirits under the exceptionally favorable conditions of monasticism; now it is a duty laid on every Christian in the world.[54]

From time to time there have been those since Luther who have argued that Christianity can be properly expressed only in a Christian commonwealth where the means of production and distribution are held in common. But the urging of people like F. D. Maurice, Bishop Barnes of Birmingham, or Hewlett Johnson, Dean of Canterbury, have not been widely accepted as a definition of the duty of 20th century Christians. The duty of Christians about property was defined by the Church of England in Article XXXVIII of the Thirty-Nine Articles of Religion: *The Riches and Goods of Christians are not common, as touching the right, title, and possession of the same; as certain Anabaptists do falsely boast. Notwithstanding, every man ought, of such things as he possesseth, liberally to give alms to the poor, according to his ability.*[55]

The notion of duty persists. The catechism says *the duty of all Christians is to follow Christ; to come together week by week for corporate worship; and to work, pray, and give for the spread of the kingdom of God.*[56] Currently, as I have stated, that duty of giving is the tithe. Ten per cent of..? Well, no one is too sure of what!

It is certainly true, whether we want to place ourselves among the disciples or in the ranks of the crowd, that Jesus was making it perfectly plain that any notion that wealth automatically produces happiness is absurd. Making money and having wealth is not as difficult as knowing what to do with it so that life is enriched![57]

Responsible stewardship, or responsible ownership, will enable life to be enriched when the institutions for the ministry of reconciliation (i.e. parishes, dioceses and the national church) are supported by the tithes of the believers and the endemic poor of our society are enabled to live through the giving of our alms. The New Testament abounds with verification of almsgiving, if not tithing.

When God gave ownership of the means of production, distribution and exchange to human beings he gave us freedom of choice. I am free to choose not to accept the responsibility of tithing or of almsgiving. That freedom can never be taken away from me.

20

IMPLICATIONS

In my parish I have a remarkably efficient, reliable, compliant and friendly assistant. Provided I give clear instructions I know that every task I assign to my assistant will be carried out with skill and accuracy. There have been times when my assistant has "forgotten" things but almost always that has been my fault. You have probably guessed I have a computer!

Computer technology has, in the space of a few years, become remarkably sophisticated. And the experts tell us that my assistant is really only a Model T! One of the tasks I can give my computer is to solve some "what if?" questions. So far, they have to be very simple questions. I am waiting for the day when my computer will be able to respond when I ask a question like, "What if all the parishioners of Good Shepherd recognized their rights and responsibilities of ownership of the world, things, and power God has deeded to them, by tithing their resources to ensure that our worship of God be the best we can offer, and giving for the enablement of the poor and disadvantaged?"

John MacNaughton reports on a study done in the Episcopal Church where it was calculated that *if every Episcopal family in the nation were suddenly to become destitute and all were to go on Social Security at the lowest family income level, and then, if all Episcopalians at that income level were to give a proportionate gift of five percent to God through the Church, the income of the Church for God's work would increase by seven times over.*[59]

My unease with the idea that we give to God in that comment is relieved somewhat with the qualifier "through the Church." What the study reveals is that, whatever or whomever is the recipient of the gift, the resources for giving are enormous!

But the answer to my "what if?" question would be even more astounding if we were to compute the resources of all human beings on the basis that all accepted the "sound theology" of stewardship as paying the tithe and giving alms.

23

Matthew Fox, the American philosopher and theologian, points to a study which showed that *the cost of providing clothing, housing, feeding, health care and education for all those who don't have it in the world would cost us seventeen billion dollars a year. That is what the human race is spending every two weeks on weapons!*

And our resources are even more formidable than that. Fox quotes Buckminster Fuller as saying, more than six years ago that *We could close down every university, library, every computer in the country and, with the knowledge and technology we now have, without knowing one word about anything, we could clothe, feed and provide sufficient health care and education for everyone in the world within two and a half years.*[60]

Of course it is idle foolishness to imagine that all humanity is going to accept the responsibilities which accompany the rights of the ownership of the world. The competing theologies of ownership make that an impossibility. What we can do is explore the implications of a theology of duty and responsibility as it applies to those who say, week after week, "I believe..." We might receive some help from looking at models that have been either tried or suggested.

The first model I have already alluded to. Let's renounce ownership of the world and the responsibilities ownership brings. Give the title back to the original owner. That's monasticism.

Another model, which is gaining in attractiveness among Muslims, is the theocracy, a nation governed by God through representatives such as priests. *Dar al Islam*, the Land of Islam, is an expression of the limited partnership between the Creator and the creation.

(The U.S.S.R.'s stewardship of ownership is based on the premise that God does not exist, so there is no partnership where all belongs to me and I belong to Christ and Christ belongs to God.)

There have been attempts to create a theocracy where the Christian understanding of right and responsibility is put into practice for, and by, everyone. In Medieval Catholicism *there was, it is true, no little conflict between Emperor and Pope, not to mention lesser lights, over concrete questions of authority and administration; but both, in principle, were prepared to believe that the will of God is the ultimate standard of all human institutions and activities...thus in the Middle*

Ages, the lordship of religion over the whole domain of human life was grandly conceived and asserted.[61]

Calvin's Geneva was an to attempt to Christianize the whole social order. There were rules for everything from grace before meals to interest rates! Theology decided the price of meat, the time a person could devote to "honest games" (presumably "dishonest games" were outlawed!), the fee to be charged for a surgical operation, and even the hour (9 p.m.) for innkeepers to put their guests to bed. Murder, adultery, blasphemy and heresy were punishable by death. Torture to obtain "confessions" was systematically employed. That was the theocratic model of Calvin for a "sound theology" of stewardship![62]

It is doubtful that England ever thought of itself as a theocracy, although the doctrine of the Divine Right of Kings comes perilously close to it. In the 1662 revision of the English Book of Common Prayer there are two rubrics dealing with stewardship, although, as in the latest Episcopal prayer book, that word is not used. In The Order for the Administration of the Lord's Supper, or Holy Communion, there is a rubric at the time for the offertory which reads, *the Deacons, Church-wardens, or other fit persons appointed for that purpose, shall receive the Alms for the Poor, and other devotions of the people, in a decent bason to be provided by the Parish for that purpose; and reverently bring it to the Priest, who shall humbly present and place it upon the holy Table.*[63] What is meant by the "other devotions of the people" is not clear, but there is no ambiguity about the alms for the poor; there is a rubric to cover what happens to them. *After the Divine Service is ended, the money given at the Offertory shall be disposed of to such pious and charitable uses, as the Minister and Church-wardens shall think fit. Wherein if they disagree, it shall be disposed of as the Ordinary [Bishop] shall appoint.*[64]

That which was received at the Offertory and presented at the altar was not used to pay the parish expenses, the heating bill or any other "need of the institution." What people gave to the institution at the Offertory (or, to God, if you are so inclined) was, in turn, given away by the institution.

How did the parish church survive? If all the money given to it was in turn given away, who kept the buildings in repair, paid for the parson and maintained other programs of the parish? The answer was a curious amalgam of patronage and taxation! Not state patronage or taxation but church taxation and patronage. The nobility, the landlords, were required to patronize the church and provide for its maintenance. That was their—dreaded word—duty. They paid their dues for their place in the social structure. They created endowments. They gave property.[65]

The nobles were obliged. This *noblesse oblige* was the tax on the wealthy, a tax which they passed on to their tenants as—yes—the tithe.

The idea of the duty of those who "have" to support the institutional life of the church, enabling it to offer the sacrifice of praise and thanksgiving to God, has survived to a very limited extent in England. In West Germany, and in some of the Scandinavian countries, it survives as the "church tax," which is a percentage of the taxes levied by the state on its citizens and passed through to the various branches of the church. This state tax is voluntary to the extent that it is possible to have a conscientious objection to paying it! The institution's responsibility is that it cannot deny the services of the church to those who pay the tax. In the United States this system survives in denominations which "expect" the tithe from their membership. I know of at least one Episcopal parish where, to be eligible to nominate for the vestry, a person must declare that he or she is either a tither or working toward that goal.

Any notion that the state could, or should, impose a church tax in this country is beyond comprehension. We do need serious debate, however, as to whether the Episcopal Church should make it an imperative for those who, Sunday by Sunday, dutifully say "I believe."

When Albert Einstein wrote on the chalkboard the earth shattering equation $E=MC^2$ he did not go on to design the Manhattan Project or the plans for nuclear power plants. His theoretical calculations opened the way for the practitioners, the technologists, to put "arms and legs" on his theory. I am disturbed that many of the manuals on stewardship education and programs offer a few pages of theology but quickly get down to the "how to" blue prints for running a successful campaign. This may be because it is assumed that sound theology on stewardship is already being taught. My suspicion is that it is more likely the expression of our concern with "doing" rather than "being."

A layman wrote recently in The Living Church a moving witness to his understanding of responsible love in regard to his possessions:

When I think about giving today, I don't concern myself much with theological concepts of gratitude or principles of stewardship, important as they are. I simply give because I love my church and I want it to go on for my children and their children in future generations, until our Lord returns. I give because I want my church to have the means to respond when someone knocks at the door — and even to reach out to those who don't know how to knock[66]

I like the comment of Anne Novak, lay parish assistant, Trinity Church, Milton, Vermont, quoted in *More Blessed to Give*. She wrote:

I believe a growing, effective stewardship to be a direct result of a growing commitment to Christ and our mission and call to be Christ-bearers. The focus then, to me, needs to be on developing spirituality rather than on stewardship. I am turned off by a list of gimmicky, clever "ways" of doing or encouraging stewardship, because any level of stewardship, no matter how high, has no particular substance if it does not spring from authentic awareness of God.[67]

Authentic awareness will proceed from deep reflection on the images and words given in Scripture, on critical assessment of the Tradition of the living community and on using our brains to seek the truth that is in both.

In a letter to me, the Rev'd John Brackett, Ph.D., a parish priest in Florida, who is attempting to think through a sound theology of stewardship, wrote that *there is no doubt that much remains to be carried out in the future to call into question the typical and often tragic tendency of New Testament commentators to theologize passages which often deal with economic issues. I think that we will be surprised when we begin to do this. We will discover that Paul and the early church talked much more about money and power than we have given them credit for.*[68]

27

This exploration began with the assertion that all Christians are theologians. I even suggested that all human beings are theologians. We have to decide who will be our mentors and from where we will find our understanding of the theology of stewardship. From the press rostrum of the White House? From the glass, stainless steel and plastic towers of Madison Avenue? From the board rooms of multi-national corporations? From the PolitBuro? From the synthetic worlds of Walt Disney or Jim Bakker? From the cynical who say "I believe" when they don't believe a word of it? Do we want to flee to our own desert and leave this "naughty world?" Do we put our efforts into electing to high office those who would make America a mirror image of Calvin's Geneva?

By not facing the issue of responsible ownership we have trivialized religion. This trivialized, "civil" religion has great appeal, but it is empty and unsatisfying. There are vast numbers in the pews of our churches who are beginning to understand that they have been cheated by an unfulfilled promise of happiness and peace given by our consumer oriented way of life.

This exploration is to bring us back to the Father God, the creator of all that is:

Thank you for giving us dominion over this world. Thank you for signing over the title deed to this marvelous universe. Thank you for giving Jesus to live and die as a human and model for my human responsibilities which go with my "human rights." Give me the grace to allow me to forsake the false, the spurious, the shallow substitutes for responsibility so often presented to me. Help me do my duty. Give me the grace to pay my dues. I believe that all this belongs to me, with others; we all belong to Jesus, and Jesus belongs to you. I desperately need your grace to be able to live that and articulate that so that your will may "be done on earth as it is in heaven."

THE ENVIRONMENT

In the beginning God created the heavens and the earth.[69]

In the beginning was the Word: and the Word was with God and the Word was God... Through him all things came to be.[70]

Those sentences are separated by more than millennia. The environment in which the Genesis writer penned the words which were read by the astronauts when they viewed the earth from the surface of the moon was vastly different from the one in which the writer of the Fourth Gospel wrote the opening words of his prologue. Understanding the words involves having some knowledge of the context, the conditions, the situations in which the words were written. Bible study which does not use that approach can degenerate into using the Bible as a kind of wishing well wherein we dip our empty bucket from time to time only to get some water to slake our thirst. That "proof text" approach might, like the water in Jacob's well at Samaria, quench thirst for a time, but only the "living water" of the incarnated Word enables us never to thirst again.[71]

I have attempted to explore some of the issues involved arriving at a sound theology of stewardship or ownership of this marvelous world. But a sound theology must be lived out in time and space.

Bishop Kenneth Cragg suggests that there are two themes implicit in a Christian approach to the responsibility of ownership: *identity in respect of its own past and openness to the life of all. For the "body of Christ" in the world is recognizable by its own recognition of humanity. Its identity in the sense of character and meaning is found by identity, in the sense of participation, with mankind... As St. Paul told the Romans... "You see your calling, brethren," he said. It is that we are "involved in mankind."*[72]

My observation is that, often, Christian people, both clergy and lay, have a decided tendency to ignore the world when it comes to dealing with "church" things and leave all their "worldly" wisdom outside the

29

door when they come into a vestry meeting! Cragg is arguing for a universalistic approach for Christianity. Some further words of his are relevant here as we look at the context of our stewardship message:

As the Christ of Galilee and Jerusalem in New Testament times became the Christ of the Mediterranean, of Athens and Rome, so the Christ of the West must more evidently be the Christ of the world. It is the conviction of Christian faith that he is only known anywhere in his fullness, when the whole world, in its cultural diversity, takes possession of him and in freedom, in thought and in form, tells of him what it learns and loves.[73]

The Hebrews lived out their understanding of the will of God, who made the the earth and gave it to humanity, first as nomads, then as slaves, then as nomads again, then as a settled people who had to learn the art of living in urbanized society. Politically they began under charismatic leaders, moved on to Law interpreted by judges, then to a monarchy and, by the time of Jesus, survived as an oppressed people with little political influence.

The environment for the church has had a similar history and now witnesses to the truth of the gospel in enormously diverse environments. Even here in the U. S. A. the complexity of the economic environment often serves to confuse radical teaching about stewardship.

Most of us work about three months of the year in what some have called "involuntary servitude" because all our resources in that time go toward the maintenance of the state. But we also live in an economic environment we call free enterprise. What Karl Marx called capitalism is the engine which drives this system. Were Paul to be with us today he would have no idea what we were talking about! In vast areas of the world Christians have to witness in an economic environment of socialism which purports to accept humanity as so important that everybody owns everything, which, in effect, means that nobody owns anything. Christians live in all these environments and they affect the way the Christian enterprise is funded.

Just as we can feel dull on a dreary wintry day and lighthearted on a sunny one, the economic environment affects the way we respond to the message of stewardship.

Many Christians, even in this country, do not give a significant proportion of their income for the work of the church (or for any other philanthropy) simply because they feel that the money they are obligated to surrender from their pay packet is enough or more than enough. All of us have faced the "before taxes" or "after taxes" question about stewardship. Having collected taxes, an argument goes, it is now the responsibility of the state to look after the less fortunate in our midst. Oddly, some who argue this way look down on those who are the beneficiaries of state welfare programs.

Turning the stewardship emphasis on its head has done much to counter this attitude, emphasizing the "need of the giver to give." Indications are, however, that this strategy is not being as effective in diocesan and national church endeavors as we had first hoped. Certainly the need of the giver to give is not sufficient motivation to garner all the resources needed to meet the needs for food, clothing, housing and education of all those who are unable to provide for themselves. In parish communities only around ten per cent of what the parish receives is given away by the parish.

One of the most important environmental factors in the whole stewardship enterprise is the matter of communication. The events of the recent past in some of the television ministries is an illustration in reverse about how poorly we communicate in the life of the parish. Vast sums of money were raised because people were told that it would go to feed the starving in some third-world country, or build a hospital, school, or allow an evangelist to preach the gospel. The evidence seems to suggest that much of the money given for those purposes was, in fact, used to pay for the air time to raise the money or, in at least one instance, to increase the personal wealth of the persons raising the money!

That is an illustration in reverse because it points up the fact that when people are presented with a real need, a real disaster, some situation of deprivation, they will give. So often in our parishes, and in our dioceses, we simply do not communicate the needs in a way

31

which touches the heart strings and the purse strings of those to whom we appeal. We also need to tell those who give exactly what has happened to their gifts. It is time to accept communication as a vital part of the stewardship enterprise.

We have all encountered the environmental factor I have come to call the "all we have" syndrome. In the incident of the feeding of the multitude when Jesus told his disciples to give the people who had come to hear him something to eat they responded with *all we have with us is five loaves and two fish.*[74] Commentators have suggested that others in the crowd had food and that, in accepting the little bit from the disciples and handing it out for all to share, Jesus shamed the people present into bringing out their own goodies and handing them around. The miracle was a miracle of sharing as much as it was a miracle of providing.

Time and again people refuse to look at their responsibilities of ownership and the need to share their resources by telling you that they are on a fixed income. "All we have." One of the most effective ways of combating that syndrome is to have those who do exercise their responsibility of sharing to witness to that fact to the whole congregation. Nobody I know who is a responsible giver has told me that they have been deprived of the necessities of life because they gave!

The "all we have" syndrome creates an environment of defeatism and leads to a survival mentality. There is a ministry waiting for those with the gift of being able to show individuals, parishes and dioceses how to break out of this survival mentality.

Professor Robert Cooper makes the valid point that stewardship is really all about conversion. What I fear most, unfaithful as I am, is that many of our parishes have allowed the environment of the market place to determine parish and diocesan life negatively. I have already lamented that so many with great fiscal expertise leave it outside the door when they come in to sit at a church business meeting. What is not left outside the door is an unwillingness to "turn around" and look at life and its living through the eyes of Jesus of Nazareth. When we are converted — born again — we are not taken out of this world. We will still live in a capitalist, free enterprise society. We will still have all the tensions of trying to find the good in the multiplicity of choices offered to us. But we will see it all in a new way.

32

The line Freddy sings in "My Fair Lady,"

> *I have often walked down this street before,*
> *but the pavement always stayed beneath my feet before,*
> *all at once am I several stories high*
> *being here on the street where you live,*

is an evangelical statement of conversion. As Christians in Russia or China are attempting to witness to the truth of the gospel in a socialist environment we must be converted to see that in our capitalism we need to be "several stories high" above the forces of whatever holds our feet to the pavement in a lifestyle that has no lasting value.

The saga of faith which began with the words *in the beginning God created the heavens and the earth* has found a way of living itself out in a multitude of environments. The miracle of conversion has been there all along. Human beings have seen what responsible love means in practical terms. Kenneth Cragg provides me with words to sum up what I am trying to say: *There are, then, in the New Testament ample precedents for what we are pondering, without devalidating, where it may be viable, the traditional pattern of intellectual credence and creed. When we invite to conversion we mean first a re-orientation of personality into the Christ dimension in practical terms.*[75]

James Fowler, in *Stages of Faith*, asks some disturbing questions:

• *What are you spending and being spent for? What commands and receives your best time, your best energy?*

• *What causes, dreams, goals or institutions are you pouring out your life for?*

• *As you live your life what power or powers do you fear or dread?*

• *To what or to whom are you committed in life? In death?*

• *With whom or what group do you share your most sacred and private hopes for your life and for the lives of those you love?*

• *What are those most sacred hopes, those most compelling goals and purposes in your life?*[76]

To ask those questions of, say, a refugee family in Ethiopia as they watch children die of malnutrition would not only be absurd, it would be cruel. But in the environment in which we live the questions are both relevant and important. One of the most difficult areas to deal with in stewardship education (and in my own life, if I'm honest with myself) is getting people living in our society to admit that they are wealthy. Because of our wealth Fowler's questions are both relevant and important. Wealth is relative, I know, but given that as fact, Americans are wealthy. Robert Samuelson in an essay in Newsweek magazine quotes from "Dollars and Dreams: The Changing American Income Distribution"[77] and points out that:

• *Between the late 1940s and the late 1960s median family incomes (adjusted for inflation) roughly doubled. In general, the increase didn't reflect two earner families. Typically, Word War II veterans had also doubled their incomes over the same period.*

• *Living standards improved dramatically. In the mid 1940s one-third of the nation's homes had no running water, two fifths had no flush toilets, three fifths had no central heating and four fifths were heated by coal or wood.*

• *Retirement—once a privilege—became routine. In the late 1940s, about half of all men over 65 still worked, while a quarter of the elderly lived with their children. Social Security meant the elderly could be independent as well as retired.*

• *Regional poverty dropped sharply. In the mid 1940s average incomes in the South were about two thirds of the national average. By 1970 Southern incomes had risen to four fifths of the national average.*[78]

I wrote earlier of the *noblesse oblige*, the obligation of the nobility, of earlier times. In the environment in which we now live we are the nobles. We now have an obligation. Our obligation is to ensure that the institutions which enable and ennoble humankind are supported from our wealth. Real conversion will be reflected in that kind of generous response to ownership. There are indications, despite the "Wall Street" movie character's credo that "greed is good," that there is fertile ground for such a message. In the same issue of Newsweek

oblige of middle class

there is an article titled "The New Volunteerism."[79] The article, in a series of anecdotes, reveals that there is a response to the gospel imperative for care and concern for those less fortunate. The words of Jesus quoted by Luke in Acts, that there is more happiness in giving than receiving,[80] is poignantly illustrated in the last anecdote:

A series of visits with a 12 year old boy suffering from leukemia left its mark on hospital volunteer Davidson. "One day I had a very tough day at the firm, and I almost didn't come to the hospital because I was so tired. When I saw him, I said, 'Boy did I have a hard day.' And he looked at me and said, 'Yeah, I had a pretty tough day, too.' Suddenly I realized that I hadn't had a tough day at all." The boy has since died. "I still have his picture," Davidson says. It's there to remind him after tough days at work.

He may not have recognized it, but Davidson was following in the footsteps of David's son!

We are the salt of the earth. We are the light set on a hill. We are blessed. In the end all the strategizing, all the theorizing, all the study and analysis comes down to the simple fact for the Christian that, as Peter exhorted the first generation of Christians, Jesus has *left an example for you to follow the way he took.*[81]

HOARDING AND GIVING

The opposite of giving is hoarding.

Oscar Carr, in 1976, wrote about wealth and property with the assumption that we are stewards rather than owners of our resources and observed that the *steward is not a hoarder or a narrowly custodial functionary.*[82] J. C. Michael Allen in the same book wrote that *neither money nor any possession at all is to be hoarded. It is not to be accumulated mindlessly...*[83]

I saw one of the best examples of mindless accumulation of wealth on a hot and dusty afternoon in upper Egypt in the same year Carr's book was published. I descended the long tunnel into the depths of a hill in the Thebes valley to visit the tomb of King Tut. The room is now empty except for the mummy case, enclosed in glass, in which lies the remains of the boy king. It was weird to stand there and look at an enormous chamber hewn out of the rock of the mountain and see on the walls the magnificent paintings which were to serve as an introduction for the king in the new world which he believed he was entering. Adjacent to the burial chamber is another large room once crammed full of all the things necessary for the boy king to sustain his life in that new world. All those artifacts are now on exhibit in the Cairo Museum. Pots and pans. Jewelry. Ornaments. Even a miniature chariot, bed and other paraphernalia reminiscent of the splendor in which Tut lived as Pharaoh. There were even seeds so that in the new life the king could plant and grow his food!

Saying that Tut's tomb is an example of mindless accumulation of wealth is a judgment made from the perspective of someone who has come to understand the meaning of life and death by living in the life and death of Jesus of Nazareth. For Tut, as with all Pharaohs, it was a sacred duty on ascending the throne to begin preparation of the tomb in which to be buried and to furnish that tomb with all that was necessary to sustain life until the day of resurrection. I have a strong suspicion, though, that there are many today who are not all that far away from Tut's philosophy concerning possessions!

My mind goes to the Thebes valley because I need to remember that my heritage as a human being began with a people who lived for centuries in the world of the Pharaohs. Even in the collective consciousness of the Hebrews there must have been an echo of that kind of attitude to possessions. On Maundy Thursday we read the saga of the Passover when the Hebrews were to fortify themselves for their journey into the new land to which God was leading them. They were to slaughter a lamb, cook it, and eat it, and they were explicitly told that they *must not leave any over until the morning: whatever is left till morning you are to burn. You shall eat it like this: with a girdle round your waist, sandals on your feet, a staff in your hand. You shall eat it hastily: it is a passover in honor of the Lord.*[84]

Surely there must have been a great temptation to stockpile some of the food! They were going out of Egypt on a journey to a Promised Land with little or no idea of where they were going and they were expected to go without food? Heaven only knew what was in store for them in the wilderness. Look at the Pharaohs. They even had food in their burial chambers for the journey into death. To expect an entire population to move with no more than the food in their bellies from last night's hastily eaten feast was absurd. Yet that was the command and that is what they did. The people who were to be a light to the nations around them had to learn from the outset that if God called them they had to trust that he would provide for them.

Unfortunately, that is not the whole story. The sacred text itself will not let me get away with such a lovely biblical illustration of the evil of hoarding. The fact is that the Hebrews did not leave Egypt empty handed; the Bible records that on the night of their departure *the people carried off their dough, still unleavened, on their shoulders, their kneading bowls wrapped in their cloaks.*[85] But there was more. They left Egypt with loot. It's right there in the text: *The sons of Israel did as Moses had told them and asked the Egyptians for silver ornaments and gold, and for clothing. The Lord gave the people such prestige in the eyes of the Egyptians, that they gave them what they had asked. So they plundered the Egyptians.*[86]

Having lived in Israel and traveled widely in Egypt I am well aware that the antipathy between the Israelis and the Egyptians goes back a very long way! Archbishop Appleton, former Metropolitan of the Middle East, told me of a humorous illustration of that fact when he called once on the Egyptian Foreign Minister. On the wall behind the minister's desk was an exquisite framed Arabic text. The Archbishop couldn't read Arabic so he asked an aide what the script was. He seemed pleased to be able to tell the Archbishop that it was a quotation from Isaiah, *Blessed be Egypt my people.*[87] The Archbishop was familiar with scripture and reminded the aide that there was more to the text. It goes on to say, *Assyria my handiwork, and Israel my inheritance.* The aide was quick to respond, "Ah yes, but you see it's a very small frame!"

All that makes it clear that when we come to strategize about giving and to denounce hoarding we need to be well aware that we come from a long history where there is a mixture of trust and suspicion, belief and doubt, hope that is always mingled with fear. "Trust in God and keep your powder dry" is by far the determining attitude for most of us. Mother Teresa and all the other saints are the exception, not the rule!

I see an illustration of this fact of life in the incident of the feeding of the multitude I mentioned earlier. The incident made such an impression on the minds of the biographers of Jesus that it is recorded in all four gospels and in Mark twice.

If the essential message of that incident for you is that Jesus was able to multiply five loaves and two fish in a miracle of feeding thousands of hungry people you may have been offended by the comment that this event is a miracle of sharing as much as it is a miracle of providing. I'm not at all sure that the episode is recorded simply to show off Jesus' ability to multiply food. The evangelists do not say that all the people were fed only with the five loaves and the two fish. Moreover I am puzzled that we should accept that Jesus would do something he refused to do when he was tempted by his own hunger in the wilderness experience following his baptism. On that occasion he refused to turn stones into bread. It hardly seems likely that on this occasion he would multiply loaves and fish!

The story of the multiplication of the loaves has meaning for me as a miracle of sharing, not a miracle of providing. From John's account of it we learn the source of those loaves and fish. They were given up by a young lad. No self-respecting Jewish mamma was going to have her boy go off for the day to follow some itinerate rabbi without providing him with his lunch! When the disciples put out the word that they wanted food it was that boy who gave up his lunch. All the rest had their provisions carefully hidden away in their clothing. When the appeal was made for food no one moved. If Isaac brought out his lunch how did he know that Jacob next to him had not been careless about bringing food for himself and his family? That would mean having to share and he would have less to eat. When Jesus took the lad's lunch, blessed it and gave it to the disciples to start handing out to the crowd they were all so ashamed of their selfishness that out came all the food, they all ate, and there was so much that twelve baskets full were left over!

A secondary implication of the story is that with planning, even planning for your own survival, there is always enough to go around with a great deal to spare.

The idea of planning, particularly planning for the responsible disposition of our goods when we no longer can exercise our ownership of them goes back a long way.

The first prayer book of the Church of England (1549) had this rubric in the Order for the Visitation of the Sick, after the dying person has made a confession of faith:

And if he hath not afore disposed of his goods, let him then make his will. (But men must be often admonished that they set an order for their temporal goods and lands, when they be in health.) And also to declare his debts, what he oweth, and what is owing to him: for discharging his conscience, and quietness of his executors.

A similar rubric now appears on page 445 of the American prayer book, at the end of the service of Thanksgiving for the Birth or Adoption of a Child. It includes an exhortation for parents to make prudent provision for the well being of their families.

The scriptural justification for that rubric goes way back to the Genesis story of Joseph's rise to power in Egypt when he bought up all the land for the Pharaoh's court. It's a fascinating story of agrarian reform in reverse. After buying up all the land of the impoverished Egyptians Joseph said to the people: *This is how we stand: I have bought you out, with your land, on Pharaoh's behalf. Here is seed for you so that you can sow the land. But when harvest comes you must give a fifth to Pharaoh. The other four fifths you can have for sowing your fields, to provide food for yourselves and your households, and food for your dependents. 'You have saved our lives' they replied. 'If we may enjoy my lord's favor, we will be Pharaoh's serfs.'* [88]

That principle of tenant farming remains to this day in the Middle East. All the agricultural land around Nablus on the West Bank of Jordan, for example, is owned by seven Nablusi families. Our government has found in its peace efforts that there are many complications when it comes to securing peace in the Middle East. Not the least has to do with this policy of land ownership.

Hebraic law for providing for children even extended to the right of ownership of other people — slavery. God did not give only the decalogue to Moses on Mount Sinai. He said this: *The servants you have, men and women, shall come from the nations round you; from those you may purchase servants, men and women. You may also purchase them from the children of the strangers who live among you, and from their families living with you who have been born on your soil. They shall be your property and you may leave them as an inheritance to your sons after you, to hold in perpetual possession.* [89]

I doubt that any of the preachers who are so insistent that we follow all the commands of God's word would be prepared to argue that as a way of providing for our children!

From the Hebrew Scriptures, the proverb: *The good man bequeaths his heritage to his children's children, the wealth of the sinner is stored up for the virtuous.* [90]

Jesus recognized this innate sense of responsibility to provide for children even in those whom he regarded as intrinsically evil. *If you, then, who are evil, know how to give your children what is good, how much more will your father in heaven give good things to those who ask him!* [91]

Honesty forces me to remind you of another saying of Jesus which seems to contradict the idea that we have a responsibility to provide for our families both from our present resources and from that which we leave to them as an inheritance. *And everyone who has left houses, brothers, sisters, father, mother, wife, children or land for the sake of my name will be repaid a hundred times over, and also inherit eternal life.* [92]

40

That sentiment is expressed somewhat differently by Luke who hears Jesus say: *If any man comes to me without hating his father, mother, wife, children, sisters, yes and his own life too, he cannot be my disciple...none of you can be my disciples unless he gives up all his possessions.*[93] Because of that text I can only claim to be a *follower* of Jesus of Nazareth, not a disciple! There are those who are still called to that kind of discipleship and for them I have enormous admiration.

Finally, in looking at the scriptural justification for a prayer book rubric which demands that we provide for our children as a way of showing responsible love, there is a word from Paul who wrote to the Corinthian Christian community of his plans to come and visit them for a third time. Apparently he had heard that the community could not really afford to pay his expenses so he wrote assuring them that he didn't expect an honorarium and, using a familial metaphor said that *children are not expected to save up for their parents, but parents for children.*[94]

That's a fascinating comment because it doesn't seem to fit with the prevailing attitude of Paul's time.

The Corinthian Christian community was composed primarily of Greeks. Even given the fact that Paul himself admitted that not many of the community were wise, influential or came from noble families,[95] it would certainly be true that some of them had been educated in Greek philosophy and manners. That education would have introduced them to Plato who, for centuries, had greatly influenced Greek life. Plato wrote: *All which a man has belongs to those who gave him birth and brought him up, and that he must do all that he can to minister to them, first, in his property, secondly, in his person, and thirdly in his soul, in return for the endless care and travail which they bestowed upon him of old, in the days of his infancy, and which he is now to pay back to them when they are old and in the extremity of their need.*[96]

About two hundred years later Aristotle wrote this: *In the matter of food we should help our parents before all others, since we owe our nourishment to them, and it is more honorable to help in this respect the authors of our being even before ourselves.*[97]

Even if it could be argued that Paul dismissed those pagan exhortations, the practice of caring for parents was deeply rooted in the

Jewish tradition. It stems from the commandment in the decalogue, *Honor your father and your mother, that your days may be long in the land which the Lord your God gives you.*[98] Jesus apparently held to this responsibility despite the passages I quoted earlier. In a dispute with the Pharisees who had found a neat loophole in the law about care for parents Jesus said this: *'You put aside the commandment of God to cling to human traditions.' And he said to them, 'How ingeniously you get around the commandment of God in order to preserve your own tradition! For Moses said: "Do your duty to your father and mother," and, "Anyone who curses father or mother must be put to death. But you say, "If a man says to his father or mother: Anything that I have that I might have used to help you is Corban (that is, dedicated to God), then he is forbidden from that moment to do anything for his father or mother." '*[99]

If nothing else those passages reveal that we need to be very careful in attempting to use the scriptural component in the trinity of Scripture, Tradition and Reason, as we try to find truth. It seems to me that there is justification for asserting that responsible love in terms of the disposition of our resources is a two-way street. It involves parental responsibility to children and children's responsibility to parents.

One of Jesus' parables deals directly with the matter of giving or hoarding. Jesus told the story when a man in a crowd asked him to force his brother to share the family inheritance. Jesus refused to arbitrate the dispute and made this penetrating comment: *Watch and be on your guard against avarice of any kind, for a man's life is not made secure by what he owns, even when he has more than he needs.*[100] To illustrate that point he told a story:

There was once a rich man who, having had a good harvest from his land, thought to himself, "What am I to do? I have not enough room to store my crops." Then he said, "This is what I will do; I will pull down my barns and build bigger ones, and store all my grain and my goods in them, and I will say to my soul: My soul, you have plenty of good things laid by for many years to come; take things easy, eat, drink, and have a good time." But God said to him, "Fool! This very night the demand will be made for your soul; and this hoard of yours, whose will it be then?" [101]

No words of mine could make the point any clearer. Unless and until the process of my conversion to the vision of reality presented in Jesus brings me to the place where I must intentionally plan for the responsible disposition of my resources, however meager they might be, I will miss the mark of God's intention for my life. That our church is offering a ministry to teach the responsibilities of steward-ship or ownership is cause for rejoicing. We may well gain additional resources to continue to be the light of the world but, that is secondary. The primary reason for us to be involved in this enterprise is that we can help human beings to become fully what they are meant to be, children of God, made in his image; children who will face that moment when we will be alone at the gate of death with calm serenity because we know in whom we have trusted, having no doubt at all that he is *able to take care of all that we have entrusted to him until that Day.*[102]

1. Dietrich Ritschl, *The Logic of Theology*, Fortress Press, Philadelphia, 1987, p. xviii.
2. John 14:6.
3. The Book of Common Prayer, p. 166.
4. *Biblical Authority or Biblical Tyranny? Scripture and the Christian Pilgrimage*, William Countryman, Fortress Press, Philadelphia, 1981, p. 110.
5. James Fowler, Harper & Row, San Francisco, 1981, pp. xi, xii.
6. Matthew 6:10.
7. Matthew 7:15-16, *The Jerusalem Bible*, Doubleday & Company Inc., New York, 1966. All quotations from scripture will be from this version unless otherwise noted.
8. John H. MacNaughton, *More Blessed to Give...*, The Episcopal Church Center, New York, 1983, p. 6.

9. Alan Richardson, *Christian Apologetics*, S.C.M. Press Ltd., London, 1950, pp. 78, 79.

10. Psalms 24:1.

11. Genesis 1:28-30.

12. Richard W. Anderson, *Creation Versus Chaos* (Philadelphia: Fortress Press) 1987, p. 177.

13. Frank Stagg, *Polarities of Man's Existence in Biblical Perspective*, Westminster Press, Philadelphia, 1973, p. 23.

14. Stagg, Op Cit. pp. 23, 24.

15. Stagg, Op. Cit. p. 33.

16. C. F. D. Moule, *Man and Nature in the New Testament*, pp.2f.

17. 1 Corinthians 3:23.

18. J. B. Phillips, *The New Testament in Modern English*, The MacMillan Co., New York, 1972.

19. Acts 5:4.

20. Ten per cent of gross production.

21. Psalm 8:5-6. This passage quoted in Hebrews (2:6-8), translates "set all things under his feet" as "You have put him in command of everything."

22. Hans-Ruedi-Weber, *Salty Christians*, Australian Council of Churches, Sydney, 1963, p. 56.

23. Bishop of Hippo, 354-430. He is one of the "Doctors of the Church." He wrote the 22 books of *City of God* between 413 and 426. His contrast of Christianity and the world became the supreme exposition of a Christian philosophy of history.

24. From Manes, 216-276 A.D., who taught that the object of the practice of religion was to release the particles of light which Satan had stolen from the world of Light and imprisoned in man's brain and that Jesus, Buddha, the Prophets, and Manes had been sent to help in this task.

25. Luke 16:1-8.

26. Ephesians 3:2.

27. Deuteronomy 5:19.

28. Genesis 13:2.

29. Genesis 14:19.

30. 1 Chronicles 29:1-16.

31. Luke 15:11-32.

32. Matthew 23:23, Luke 11:42 and Hebrews 7:4.

33. MacNaughton, 1983, p. 53.

34. Acts 20:35.

35. Matthew 17:24-27.

36. Joachim Jeremias, *Jerusalem in the Time of Jesus*, Fortress Press, Philadelphia, 1984, pp. 105 ff.

37. Jeremias, 1984, p. 108.

38. Acts 2:44-45.

39. Jeremias 1984, p. 130.

40. Acts 15:28-29.

41. To question the use of the term "tithe" does not mean that the word is inappropriate.

Any theology which sees proportionate and systematic sharing of resources needs to begin with the tithe as a *minimum*. The analysis in this chapter is offered as part of the dialogue needed to discover a sound theology for resource sharing.

42. Josephus, *Antiquities*, 15.309.

43. Jeremias, 1984, p. 130.

44. Luke 6:20.

45. Matthew 5:1.

46. Luke 6:20.

47. Luke 6:24.

48. Anchor Bible, Matthew, Doubleday & Co. Inc., New York, 1978, p. 45.

49. 1 QM xiv 7.

50. Gerd Theissen, *Sociology of Early Palestine Christianity*, translated by John Bowden, Fortress Press, Philadelphia, 1978, points out that St. Peter says on behalf of all the disciples, "See, we have left everything and followed you" (Mark 10:28). He goes on to point out that this also applies to the seven in Jerusalem (Acts 6:5f.) and the five in Antioch (Acts 13:1f.) and that Luke also records the sending out of seventy wandering charismatics, who had to follow the same rules as the twelve Apostles (Luke 10:1 ff.; 9:1ff). p. 33.

51. Acts 2:44-45.

52. Acts 4:36-37.

53. Acts 5:1-11.

54. Deitrich Bonhoeffer, *The Cost of Discipleship*, S.C.M. Press, London, 1964, pp. 39-40.

55. The Book of Common Prayer, Seabury Press, New York, 1976, p.876.

56. The Book of Common Prayer, p. 856.

57. Much of the foregoing is reprinted (with modifications) from *The Pursuit of Happiness*, by the author, Forward Movement Publications, Cincinnati, 1987.

58. The Book of Common Prayer, p. 427.

59. MacNaughton, 1983, p. 63.

60. Transcribed from an audio tape #18: *Money and Spirituality*, Bear and Co. Inc., P.O. Drawer 2860, Sante Fe, NM 87504, 1986.

61. Ernest Fremont Tittle, *Christians in an UnChristian Society*, Hazen Books on Religion, distributed by, Association Press, New York, 1939, pp. 48ff.

62. The Rev'd Robert Cooper, Professor of Christian Ethics at The Episcopal Theological Seminary of the Southwest, suggests that this comment about Calvin craves some balance: *I do not know of a theologian—apart from Karl Barth—who more than Calvin emphasizes gift in his theological enterprise. There are many awful true things to be found in Calvin along with some horrors, but his sense of gift is something admirable in my opinion.* (From a letter to the author, September 29th, 1986.)

63. The Book of Common Prayer and Administration of the Sacraments and other rites and ceremonies of the Church according to the use of The Church of England, University Press, Oxford, p. 263.

64. The Book of Common Prayer (1662), p. 281.

65. At one time more than a third of the land of Great Britain was owned by the church.

45

66. Sidney Galloway, attorney and Senior Warden, St. Paul's Church Shreveport, La., The Living Church, The Living Church Foundation, Milwaukee Wis. Vol. 196, No. 3, January 17th, 1988 p. 11.

67. MacNaughton, 1983, p. 75.

68. John Brackett, a letter to the author, June 1986.

69. Genesis 1:1.

70. John 1:1, 2.

71. John 4.

72. Kenneth Cragg, *Christianity in World Perspective*, Lutterworth Press, London, 1968, pp. 193, 194.

73. Op Cit., p. 195.

74. Matthew 14:17.

75. Op. Cit., p. 216.

76. Fowler, Op. Cit., p. 3.

77. Russell Sage Foundation, New York, N.Y.

78. Samuelson, Robert J., Newsweek Inc., The Washington Post Co., New York, N.Y., February 8th, 1988, p. 49.

79. Op. Cit., p. 42-43.

80. Acts 20:35.

81. 1 Peter 2:21.

82. Oscar C. Carr Jr., *Jesus, Dollars and Sense*, The Seabury Press, New York, 1976, p. 16.

83. J. C. Michael Allen in an essay in *Jesus, Dollars and Sense*, op cit, p. 26.

84. Exodus 12:10-11.

85. Exodus 12:34.

86. Exodus 12:35, 36.

87. Isaiah 19:25.

88. Genesis 47:23-25.

89. Leviticus 25:44-45a.

90. Proverbs 13:22.

91. Matthew 7:11.

92. Matthew 19:29.

93. Luke 14:26, 33.

94. 2 Corinthians 12:14b.

95. 1 Corinthians 1:26.

96. Plato, Laws, IV, 717A.

97. Aristotle, Ethics, 1165.21.

98. Exodus 20:15.

99. Mark 7:9-12.

100. Luke 12:15.

101. Luke 12:16-20.

102. See 2 Timothy 1:12.